LISTEN to the EARTH

Carme Lemniscates

TILBURY HOUSE PUBLISHERS

The Earth shines like a blue jewel
in the immense, dark universe.
It is our home.

The Earth feeds us.
It has nourished us through the long, long ages.

The Earth shelters us.
When we need wood to build houses,
it gives us trees.

But the Earth needs our help to grow more trees than we cut.

When we need to warm
or cool our homes,
the Earth gives us fuel to burn.

But we're burning too much coal,
oil, and natural gas.

And the Earth gives us fuel for our vehicles
so we can zoom from place to place.
But we are using too much.

When we use resources faster than
the Earth can make more,
and when we produce more waste than
the Earth can absorb, we are borrowing
from our precious planet's future.

If we go on borrowing,
the time will come when it is too late
to repay that debt.

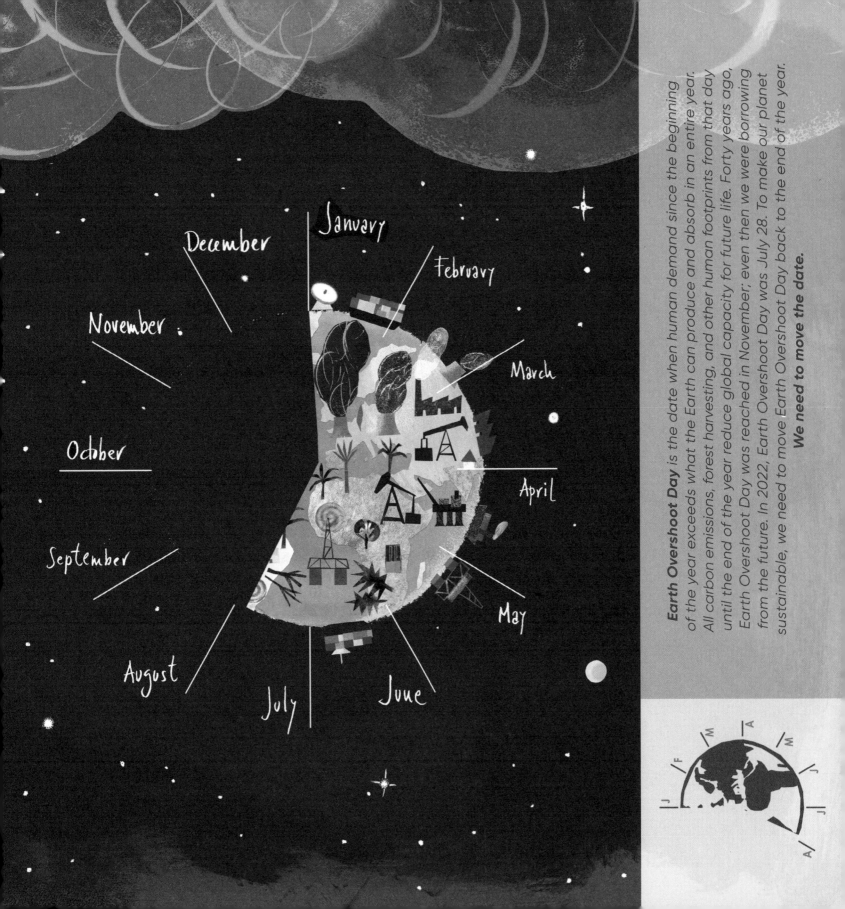

Earth Overshoot Day is the date when human demand since the beginning of the year exceeds what the Earth can produce and absorb in an entire year. All carbon emissions, forest harvesting, and other human footprints from that day until the end of the year reduce global capacity for future life. Forty years ago, Earth Overshoot Day was reached in November; even then we were borrowing from the future. In 2022, Earth Overshoot Day was July 28. To make our planet sustainable, we need to move Earth Overshoot Day back to the end of the year. **We need to move the date.**

We can find a balance.
The Earth whispers the way
to hearts that listen.

To move the date, we need to reduce our global footprint. We need to use fewer resources, leaving more for future life, and generate less waste so that the Earth can absorb what we produce. And the good news is that we already know how.

One way is to use and throw away less plastic. Think of those plastic bags we see everywhere. If we stop using them, we reduce our plastic pollution footprint and we also reduce the greenhouse gases that are generated by making plastic. **If we stop using plastic bags and packaging, we will move the date.**

When we listen,
we can find sustainable ways
to move and travel.

Transportation causes a large share of global carbon emissions.

We can replace petroleum-powered vehicles with ones that run on electric power. We can promote bicycle infrastructure in cities to encourage the use of bikes, ebikes, and cargo bikes for short trips.

For longer trips, we can replace airplane fuel with renewable hydrogen fuel. **If we shift to clean power for transportation, we will move the date.**

When we listen,
we know how to make clean energy
for healthy, sustainable cities.

Green hydrogen, or hydrogen produced with clean renewable energies, can replace fossil fuels in industrial processes and manufacturing.

Renewable energy sources, such as solar and wind power, can replace coal- and gas-fired power plants.

We can store solar and wind power in batteries when the sun shines and the wind blows, then use the power when we need it.

If we shift to these clean energies to generate the electricity we need, we will move the date.

We know how to grow new forests
and preserve habitats
for the plants and animals on Earth.

Many forests have been converted to grasslands for cattle or damaged by massive clear-cutting.

Forests are essential to the planet's health.

Reforestation increases biodiversity, absorbs carbon dioxide, regulates the climate, and preserves plants and animals.

Forests and other vibrant natural ecosystems give us beauty and well-being.

If we reforest, we will move the date.

We know how to grow and harvest food
so the Earth can keep nourishing us,
now and in the future.

We need clean air and water and fertile soil to provide healthy food. We can practice regenerative agriculture—crop rotation, green manures, compost, cover crops, and organic production—to improve the biocapacity of agricultural lands. These practices rebuild topsoil, increase soil carbon sequestration, and restore soil biodiversity. Supporting local small-scale food producers reduces "miles to market," gives jobs to people, makes us healthier, and sustains nature. **If we shift to these agriculture practices, we will move the date.**

When we listen, we know how to be wise guardians
of this precious planet we share.
We know how to care for the Earth so the Earth can care for us.

Author's Note

My gratitude to the Global Footprint Network for all the information
it has provided to help us protect our planet.
I have drawn extensively on the Global Footprint Network website at
www.footprintnetwork.org
while creating this book.

Publisher's Note: How We Can Move the Date

How do we make our precious planet sustainable? Each of us can help: Every tree we plant,
every car ride we don't take, every plastic bag we don't use, every meat dish we replace with
a plant-based food, every cardboard box we recycle, every degree we turn down the thermostat,
every energy-hungry appliance we replace with something more efficient, every light we turn off when
we leave a room—it all helps. To measure your personal ecological footprint, try the quiz at
www.footprintcalculator.org
But a global challenge needs global solutions, too. Organizations like the Global Footprint Network
(**www.footprintnetwork.org**) and Project Drawdown (**https://drawdown.org**) are pointing the way
with solutions like the ones in the following pages.
Some of these solutions will be hard to implement. Some of them overlap with others. But the good news
is that we know how to do all of them, and together they would move Earth Overshoot Day from July 28, where
it was in 2022, all the way to the end of the year or beyond, which is what our Earth needs to be sustainable.
We can do it!

Changing How We Use Plastics

can move Earth Overshoot Day a significant though still uncalculated number of days

Recycling plastic products: Production of plastics has increased more than any other human-made material since the mid-twentieth century. Most plastics are made from fossil fuel, and much of the energy required to produce and process plastic comes from burning coal. Plastic production is the planet's fifth largest generator of greenhouse gases. Reducing our "plastic footprint" will reduce energy demand and waste streams.

Ending single-use plastic: About 40% of plastic is packaging, a likely first target for regulation. Manufacturers could be required to pay into a cleanup fund or collect used plastic. There is no estimate yet for how much these actions would move the date, but it would be significant. In addition, we now know that the impacts of plastic waste on nature and human health are far-reaching.

Changing How We Travel and Ship Things

can move Earth Overshoot Day as much as 70 days

Diesel-fueled trucks contribute 4% of global carbon emissions. Stricter emissions standards and alternative fuels for trucks around the world would **move the date 1.4 days** and reduce harmful air pollution too.

Family cars cause more carbon emissions than trucks. Cities around the world are starting carshare programs that make electric cars easy to rent when they're needed for errands. The cars are located, unlocked, and paid for with a smartphone and reduce a household's transportation emissions by 4 to 18%.
Wide adoption of urban carshare programs would **move the date 3 days**.

Confining automobile through-traffic to every second or third street of urban street grids would open half to two-thirds of urban road space to pedestrians, bikes, parks, and public transit.
These superblocks would **move the date 5 days**.

Charging tolls or congestion fees on cars driven within city limits would encourage use of more energy-efficient transportation and has been shown to reduce car traffic by 22%.
Widespread implementation of congestion fees would **move the date 5 days**.

Limiting the space for parking vehicles in cities makes streets more pedestrian- and bicycle-friendly and encourages use of more energy-efficient transportation. This has the potential to **move the date 10 days**.

Why don't we slow down? Ships and cars burn less fuel when they move more slowly. Reducing the average speed of cargo ships would **move the date 0.9 day**, and reducing speed limits for cars around the world would **move the date 0.6 day**.

Cutting global automobile-driving mileage in half by walking, biking, and using public transportation would **move the date 13 days**.

Shifting from gas-powered to electric vehicles around the globe would **move the date 2.5 days**.

Replacing one-third of airplane fuel and one-half of the fossil fuels burned by industry with "green" hydrogen (hydrogen produced with renewable energy) would **move the date 18 days**. The technology exists, though it is not yet known how much fossil fuel can be replaced by hydrogen versus fossil fuel.

Replacing 50% of air travel with high-speed rail would **move the date 1.8 days**.

Widespread adoption of electric bicycles, or ebikes, for commuting could reduce car use by 15% and push back Earth Overshoot Day **4 days** if accompanied by expanded bicycle infrastructure.

Use of cargo bikes for carrying groceries and other cargoes could **move the date 2.4 days** with expanded bicycle infrastructure.

Safe and efficient bicycle infrastructure encourages more people to choose bicycles over other modes of transportation and could increase the proportion of bicycle trips up to 35% of all trips. That would **move the date 9 days**.

If we vacation closer to home, reducing the ecological footprint of air travel for tourism by half would **move the date 1 day**.

Changing How We Live, Work, and Get Electrical Power
can move Earth Overshoot Day as much as 200 days

Powering rural homes around the world self-sufficiently—with solar-powered microgrids instead of big electric utility grids and diesel generators—would **move the date 8 days**.

Over 36% of families around the world live in apartment buildings. Upgrading the insulation, lighting, heating, ventilation, and air-conditioning in multi-family apartment buildings around the world would **move the date 5 days**.

Retrofitting single-family homes with better insulation, windows, air seals, and heat-recovery systems to reduce heating and cooling demands would **move the date 7 days**.

Replacing home furnaces with electric heat pumps in cooler regions of the world would **move the date 2 days**.

Designing cities so that residents can meet most of their needs (shops, parks, schools, etc.) within a 15-minute walk or bike ride would **move the date 11 days**.

Eliminating direct emissions from buildings by adopting electric heating, electric stoves, and heat pumps would **move the date 4 days**.

Reducing air-conditioning demand with "cool roofs" (roofs that are coated white to reflect sunlight) would **move the date 0.4 day**.

Replacing wood- and charcoal-burning cookstoves around the world with electric, solar-powered, and efficient gas-powered stoves would **move the date 6 days**.

Choosing energy-saving cooking appliances such as smaller refrigerators, electric (instead of gas) stoves, and pressure-cookers could reduce energy use by one-third in the planet's high-income-region households and **move the date 0.9 day**.

Replacing home appliances with energy-efficient models can reduce home energy use by 30% and **move the date 6 days**.

Making concrete with recycled building materials instead of newly quarried sand and gravel would reduce the world's largest waste stream—the 6 billion tons of demolition waste produced each year—and **move the date 2.4 days**.

Buildings designed to suit their landscapes and local weather are easier to heat and cool, and the use of local building materials is less resource-intensive than modern concrete and steel construction. Employing design principles inspired by traditional and indigenous architecture could **move the date 11 days**.

Green roofs decrease the amount of energy needed for heating and cooling by providing improved insulation, reducing thermal fluctuations on the roof surface, and through evaporative cooling. In addition to reducing energy consumption, green roofs can increase rainwater retention and improve biodiversity. Covering half of roof areas with living vegetation would **move the date 1.6 days**.

Methane is 28 times more potent as a greenhouse gas than carbon dioxide. If 50% of the 3,000 methane-emitting coal mines worldwide were to capture and burn their methane, we could **move the date 2 to 4.5 days**.

"Smart" cities use existing technologies to reduce the energy consumption of buildings and industrial processes, encourage solar-powered homes, increase the efficiency of electricity distribution, and cut dependence on energy-intensive transportation. If applied worldwide, this could **move the date 29 days**.

Taxing carbon emissions at $100 per ton of carbon—the estimated true cost of carbon pollution—would disincentivize high-polluting activities and **move Earth Overshoot Day by 63 days**.

Producing electricity with wind turbines instead of coal, oil, and natural gas has the potential to **move the date 11.2 days** (10 days for onshore turbines; 1.2 days for offshore turbines).

Widespread use of rooftop solar panels would **move the date 5 days**.

Widespread availability of massive battery banks to store energy from solar panels and wind turbines could **move the date an additional 15 days** beyond what the adoption of renewable energy without storage would do.

Using geothermal energy to heat buildings and generate electricity would **move the date 0.8 day**.

Blending clean-burning hydrogen with natural gas for home use would **move the date 0.9 day**.

Residents of densely settled cities are less likely to drive and can be more efficiently served by electrical, water, and wastewater utilities. Avoiding sprawl by building new housing in existing urban areas rather than suburban or rural areas would **move the date 12 days**.

Using lending libraries to rent tools, appliances, recreation equipment, and other portable, long-lasting products could reduce their global consumption by one-third and **move the date 3 days**.

Air-drying laundry could reduce household dryer usage by 75% and **move the date 1.3 days**.

Universal adoption of LED lighting would **move the date 1.8 days**.

If all the world's people would dress warmly for cold weather and coolly for hot weather, we could **move the date 3 days**.

Changing How We Care for Trees
can move Earth Overshoot Day as much as 18 days

Because trees draw carbon from the atmosphere and store it in living biomass, creating tree plantations on abandoned crop, pasture, and mining lands could **move the date 3 days**.

Raising livestock on small-scale farms that mix trees and forests with grasslands would sequester large amounts of carbon dioxide while also supporting local ecosystems, communities, and traditional cultural heritages. This would **move the date 5 days**.

Widespread tree intercropping—growing trees with other crops—can protect against erosion, flooding, or wind damage and improve soil quality and crop yields in addition to sequestering carbon and **moving the date 2.1 days**.

Planting urban trees to cool cities and reduce the need for air conditioning would **move the date 0.9 day**.

Restoring and protecting tropical forests can **move the date 7 days**.

Changing How We Eat

can move Earth Overshoot Day as much as 31 days

Peatlands store carbon. Based on scenarios calculated by Project Drawdown, land management and conservation plans for peatlands can **move the date 4 days**.

Grazing plays an important role in maintaining the carbon-rich soils of grassland and prairie ecosystems. Adoption of managed grazing—controlling the timing and intensity of livestock grazing to optimize grassland soil health and enhance carbon sequestration—could **move the date 2.2 days**.

Because meat production (especially beef production) is so much more energy-intensive than plant production, eliminating meat consumption one day per week would **move the date 1.8 days**.

If we replace 50% of global meat consumption with plant-based substitutes, we will **move the date 7 days** from CO_2 and land-use alone. (If we include methane emissions, the impact is even greater.)

Regenerative agriculture practices include reduced tillage; compost application; and use of cover crops, crop rotation, and green manures to increase soil carbon sequestration, restore degraded soil biodiversity, and rebuild topsoil. Widespread adoption of these practices could **move the date 1.9 days**.

If we cut food waste in half worldwide, we would **move the date 13 days**.

Buying locally produced food reduces transportation of foods (which accounts for about 11% of carbon emissions associated with food production), strengthens local economies, and supports sustainable agriculture. If we source 80% of our food locally, we can **move the date 1.6 days**.

We can do it!

For my father.
C.L

Hardcover ISBN 978-1-958394-04-5

Library of Congress Control Number: 2022948292

Tilbury House Publishers • Thomaston, Maine
www.tilburyhouse.com

Printed in Canada

23 24 25 26 27 28 TC 10 9 8 7 6 5 4 3 2 1

Carme created this book's mixed-media illustrations with monotypes, watercolors, acrylics and collage.
www.lemniscates.com

FSC
www.fsc.org
MIX
Paper | Supporting
responsible forestry
FSC® C011825